info buzZ

The United Kingdom

Izzi Howell

W

FRANKLIN WATTS
LONDON · SYDNEY

Franklin Watts
First published in Great Britain in 2018 by The Watts Publishing Group
Copyright © The Watts Publishing Group, 2018

Produced for Franklin Watts by
White-Thomson Publishing Ltd
www.wtpub.co.uk

ISBN: 978 1 4451 5954 6
10 9 8 7 6 5 4 3 2 1

Credits
Series Editor: Izzi Howell
Series Designer: Rocket Design (East Anglia) Ltd
Designer: Clare Nicholas
Literacy Consultant: Kate Ruttle

The publisher would like to thank the following for permission to reproduce their pictures: Getty: Leonid Andronov title page and 6, fotoVoyager 8–9b, oversnap 9tr, danaibe12 10, ALLEKO 12, ADRIAN DENNIS/AFP 15r, Wendy Connett 16r, lefteyephotoguy 19l, prasit chansarekorn 19r; Shutterstock: Samot cover and 11, Alfonso de Tomas 4l, railway fx 4r, Peter Hermes Furian 5, evenfh 7t, Mcimage 7c, Billy Stock 7b, Thierry Maffeis 9tl, Fanfo 13tl, stockcreations 13tr, D. Pimborough 13bl, Gordon Bell 13br, PJ photography 14, Dean Clarke 15l, mattxfoto 16l, DiegoMariottini 17, Martin Prochazkacz 18, Leonard Zhukovsky 20, Featureflash Photo Agency 21l, Dfree 21r.

Every attempt has been made to clear copyright. Should there be any inadvertent omission please apply to the publisher for rectification.

Printed in China

Franklin Watts
An imprint of
Hachette Children's Group
Part of The Watts Publishing Group
Carmelite House
50 Victoria Embankment
London EC4Y 0DZ

An Hachette UK Company
www.hachette.co.uk
www.franklinwatts.co.uk

All words in **bold** appear in the glossary on page 23.

Contents

Where is the UK?

The United Kingdom (UK) is a **country**. It is in **Europe**.

This is the flag of the UK.

The UK has sea all around it.

UK

Europe

Which countries can you find on the map?

There are four countries in the UK. They are England, Scotland, Wales and Northern Ireland.

The UK is near to Ireland and France. ▼

Scotland

Edinburgh

Northern Ireland

Belfast

IRELAND

UNITED KINGDOM

Wales

England

Cardiff

LONDON

FRANCE

Capital cities

Each country in the UK has its own **capital city**. London is the capital city of England and the UK. It is also the biggest city in the country.

▼ Many of the UK's **laws** are made in the Houses of Parliament in London.

◀ Edinburgh is the capital city of Scotland.

Belfast is the capital city of Northern Ireland. ▼

Cardiff is the capital city of Wales.

Countryside

There are high mountains in the north and west of the UK. Some people like to climb them.

▼ This girl is **hiking** near Ben Nevis in Scotland. Ben Nevis is the highest mountain in the UK.

Have you ever climbed a hill or mountain? What could you see from the top?

The UK has a long **coast**. Some parts of the coast have sandy beaches. Others have tall rocky **cliffs**.

People like to visit this sandy beach in Wales.

▲ The Giant's Causeway is made of large blocks of stone. It is by the sea in Northern Ireland.

Interesting places

There are many interesting things to see in the UK. Stonehenge is a circle of large stones in the southwest of England.

▼ Stonehenge was built over four thousand years ago.

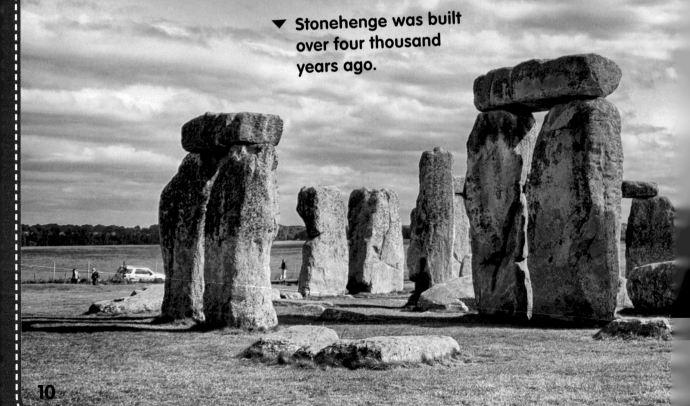

In the past, people built huge castles across the UK. Kings and important people lived in the castles.

▲
Many tourists visits Conwy Castle in Wales every year.

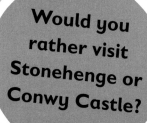

Would you rather visit Stonehenge or Conwy Castle?

Food and drink

In the UK, some people start the day with a big breakfast. They eat eggs, bacon, baked beans and toast.

Some big breakfasts also have mushrooms and tomatoes.

What do you eat for breakfast?

Some parts of the UK
have special **local** foods.

haggis (meat cooked
with oats) in Scotland ▶

◀ cawl (meat and vegetable
soup) in Wales

scones with cream
and jam in England ▶

◀ potato bread in
Northern Ireland

Sport

Some people play cricket in the summer. Cricket players usually wear white clothes.

This cricket team is playing in a field in their village.
▼

Many people like playing football in the UK.
They also watch football matches in
stadiums and on TV.

Football teams
from the UK, such
as England, play
other teams from
around the world. ▶

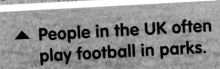

▲ People in the UK often
play football in parks.

Which sports
do you like
to play and
watch?

Festivals

People **celebrate** different festivals across the UK. On 1 March, it is St David's Day in Wales. People dance and sing Welsh songs.

These girls are wearing **traditional** Welsh hats and clothes for St David's Day. ▶

▲ These children in England are dancing around a maypole. They are celebrating May Day on 1 May.

In Scotland, they celebrate Hogmanay on New Year's Eve. Some people invite guests to parties in their homes. Other people celebrate in the street.

▼ At Hogmanay, they set off fireworks at midnight. This celebrates the new year.

When do you see fireworks?

Wildlife

Animals such as deer, rabbits and squirrels live in parks and woodlands in the UK. They eat fruit and leaves.

▼ Badgers spend most of the day in underground tunnels. They come out to find food at night.

Birds live in different **habitats** in the UK. Blackbirds and pigeons live in towns and cities. Swans and ducks live on ponds and rivers.

▼ Puffins live on cliffs near the sea.

Have you seen any of these animals before? Where did you see them?

Pheasants live in fields.

People

Some people from the UK are **famous** around the world. Andy Murray is a tennis player. He has won many prizes.

Andy Murray was the best tennis player in the world for nearly a year. ▶

Adele is a UK singer. People around the world listen to her songs. ▶

John Boyega is a UK actor. He is in the Star Wars films. ▼

Do you know any other famous people from the UK?

Quiz

Test how much you remember.

Check your answers on page 24.

1 What are the four countries in the UK?

2 What is the capital city of the UK?

3 What is the tallest mountain in the UK?

4 On which day is St David's Day?

5 Where do puffins live?

6 Which sport does Andy Murray play?

Glossary

capital city – the city where a country's government meet and work

celebrate – to do something fun on a special day

cliff – high rock with a steep side, often near the sea

coast – the land next to the sea

country – an area of land that has its own government

Europe – a continent that includes countries such as the UK, France and Spain

famous – known and recognised by many people

habitat – an area where an animal or plant usually lives

hiking – walking in the countryside

laws – the rules of a country that everyone has to follow

local – from one area

stadium – an open area with seats where sports matches take place

tourist – someone who comes to visit a place for fun

traditional – describes something that has been done in the same way for many years

Index

Answers:

1: England, Scotland, Wales and Northern Ireland; 2: London; 3: Ben Nevis; 4: 1 March; 5: On cliffs by the sea; 6: Tennis

Teaching notes:

Children who are reading Book band Purple or above should be able to enjoy this book with some independence. Other children will need more support.

Before you share the book:

• Show children different world maps and globes. Ensure they understand that blue represents sea and other colours show the land.

• Can children identify the UK on the map/globe?

• Talk about what they already know about the UK.

While you share the book:

• Help children to read some of the more unfamiliar words.

• Talk about the questions. Encourage children to make links between their own experiences and the information in the book.

• Compare the information about different places with the locality in which your school is. What is the same? What is different?

After you have shared the book:

• Help children to find where they live on different kinds of maps.

• On a large map of the UK, identify places that pupils have visited or where their relatives live.

• Work through the free activity sheets at www.hachetteschools.co.uk

Countries

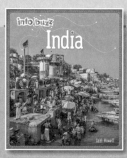

Argentina

978 1 4451 5958 4

Where is Argentina?
Cities
Countryside
Interesting places
Food and drink
Sport
Festivals
Wildlife
People

India

978 1 4451 5960 7

Where is India?
Cities
Countryside
Weather
Interesting places
Food
Sport
Festivals
Wildlife

Japan

978 1 4451 5956 0

Where is Japan?
Cities
Countryside
Interesting places
Food
Sport
Festivals
Wildlife
Art

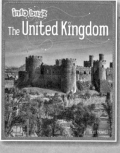

The United Kingdom

978 1 4451 5954 6

Where is the UK?
Capital cities
Countryside
Interesting places
Food and drink
Sport
Festivals
Wildlife
People

Islam

Religion

Christianity
978 1 4451 5962 1
Hinduism
978 1 4451 5964 5
Islam
978 1 4451 5968 3
Judaism
978 1 4451 5966 9

Queen Elizabeth II

History

Neil Armstrong
978 1 4451 5948 5
Queen Elizabeth II
978 1 4451 5886 0
Queen Victoria
978 1 4451 5950 8
Tim Berners-Lee
978 1 4451 5952 2

Paramedics

People who help us

Doctors
978 1 4451 6493 9
Firefighters
978 1 4451 6489 2
Paramedics
978 1 4451 6495 3
Police Officers
978 1 4451 6491 5

FRANKLIN WATTS